I0518476

Living Alongside Chronic Pain

Affirmations for Your Journey

Julie Gruber

Living Alongside Chronic Pain: Affirmations for Your Journey

For permission requests, contact www.thewordwiseproject.com

ISBN: 979-8-9993780-0-2
eISBN: 979-8-9993780-1-9

1. Self-Help 2. Self-Help Acceptance 3. Affirmations

Editing and design by Jen Pavich

Dedicated to all the brave people out there living with chronic pain.
I see you. You are not alone. And you matter.

Contents

Introduction

If you're holding this book, chances are you're navigating life with chronic pain. Maybe the pain is new and disorienting. Maybe it's been with you for years, like an unwelcome companion. Either way, I see you. And I honor the effort it takes simply to keep going.

This book was born out of my own journey with chronic pain. Over time, I came to understand that healing doesn't always mean "fixing" or erasing the pain—but it can mean softening around it, learning from it, and living more gently alongside it. Words became one of my most powerful tools. The

right words at the right moment
offered me grounding, courage, and
the kind of compassion I didn't
know I was allowed to give myself.
The affirmations in these pages are
not meant to dismiss your
experience or encourage toxic
positivity. They're here to offer small
moments of support—reminders
that your worth isn't diminished by
your pain, and that your story is still
unfolding, still yours to shape.
You might choose to read one
affirmation each morning or flip to a
random page when you're
struggling. You might move through
the book thematically, pausing to
reflect, or use it as a gentle
companion before sleep. However
you use it, I hope these words serve

as an anchor, a hand to hold, and a whisper of hope on even the hardest days.

Let's rewrite our story with chronic pain—one word, one breath, one day at a time.

Please note that while these affirmations can be a helpful supplement to your daily well-being practices, they are not intended as a substitute for professional medical or other therapeutic care.

Section 1

Grounding &
Centering

When everything feels
uncertain, I come back to
the breath.

It's not a cure, but it's a
place to land.

You are not alone in this experience.

Although we can feel lonely and isolated, we are in the company of millions upon millions of others who understand what this experience feels like.

How might you take comfort in knowing that you're not alone in this?

Reminder: BREATHE.

Pain can sometimes trick us into holding or restricting our breath.

Are you breathing normally now? Are you tensing up, or is your breathing steady and calm?

How can you remind yourself to take full, healing breaths throughout the day?

Remind your nervous
system that you are safe.

*Pain can sometimes make us feel
panic or agitation.*

*In what ways can you assure
yourself of your safety? Look
around you, look within, and
breathe into a sense of safety and
calm. What kind of safety can you
believe firmly in at this moment?*

Calm words, calm voices, calmness all around.

A sense of calm within us and around us can be soothing to our minds and bodies when we need it most.

What does "calm" sound like for you? How can you bring a sense of calmness to your voice and to your surroundings today?

Observe your thoughts and feelings without judgment.

Notice your thoughts being there without trying to push them away. Observe your feelings, give them a name, and allow them to be there too. They deserve your acknowledgement.

How might you find time today to simply observe what's happening within you?

Observe yourself without judgment.

We can be quick to judge ourselves and impose conditions on our worth.

What might it feel like to bear witness to yourself, just as you are, and see perfection there?

How might you find unconditional acceptance and love for yourself today?

Be the embodiment of
PEACE.

*Imagine yourself as the picture of
contentedness and let that
emanate outward. Despite the
pain, a sense of peace and inner
stillness is still there within you,
just waiting for you to remember
it.*

*How might you embody sincere
peace and gentleness today?*

Practice mindful awareness of what *is*.

Pain can sometimes send our thoughts spinning between future and past. Bring yourself back to this very moment and simply notice what you perceive around you, what life situation is before you, and just be in awareness of that.

What does that awareness look like for you today? How does that feel?

Calm is greater than fear.

Intentional calmness is a powerful tool against fear or worry. We can bring ourselves into the space of calm through mindful breathing, observation and presence.

How might you challenge any fear or concerns with a reassuring sense of calm today?

Ask yourself: What might the pain be trying to teach you?

Prioritizing yourself and your own well-being, setting healthy boundaries, a polished sense of discernment...there are hidden gems in this experience if we can be open to the pain becoming a wise teacher, acting on our behalf.

How might you reframe this experience and open to this possibility?

Release tension and constriction in your body.

Pain can make us tense and tighten throughout our bodies. Notice any additional constriction and breathe into it, letting your body soften and relax.

Where is there additional tension in your body right now?

Release tension and constriction in your mind.

Our brows might furrow as our minds absorb the tension stuck in thoughts and worries. Take a deep breath, notice the busy-ness of your mind, and let the constriction transform into ease.

Are your brows furrowed right now? How might you release tension in your mind today?

Section 2

*Self-Compassion &
Worth*

*Learning to treat myself
with the kindness I once
reserved for others
changed everything.*

*Not overnight—but over
time.*

Exchange negative self-talk for words of love and appreciation.

"You are so brave."

"You're trying so hard, and I'm so proud of you."

"I think you're amazing."

How will you offer yourself love and appreciation today? How can you commit to doing that more often?

Acknowledge your RELEVANCE.

You have such value, worth, and relevance in this world, and the pain cannot take that away from you. Offer yourself the recognition and acknowledgement you deserve.

What will that look like for you today, and always?

You are worthy of your devotion.

Prioritizing yourself and your well-being is an act of profound love and compassion.

In what ways can you devote energy toward yourself today? How might you reclaim your worthiness of such devotion?

Speak only kind and compassionate words to yourself.

Many of us have a feisty inner critic. It can be tempting to let that critic become our primary inner voice.

How might you challenge self-criticism with a different inner voice today, one that speaks to you with love, kindness, and compassion?

You are loved. (You truly are.)

It's not just an empty platitude. You are loved, appreciated, and valued. How can you find ways to remind yourself of that today? Think of all the people who love you, your pet(s), and all the stars in the heavens… Your presence is a miracle and a blessing.

Give yourself grace and compassion.

It's okay to have harder days, and it's okay to feel what you're feeling. How might you offer yourself some grace and compassion today for all you've been through and how hard you're working through the challenges of this experience?

How can you treat yourself with more gentleness?

Acknowledge your bravery, your strength, and your courage.

This has been a challenging set of circumstances, and you've overcome so much. Your perseverance has probably shown you that you possess more bravery, inner strength, fortitude, and courage than you ever knew you had.

How might you honor and acknowledge this today?

You are entitled to joy.

It is possible to have a joyful life, despite the presence of chronic pain. Sometimes, the sources of that joy are right in front of you, and sometimes we create it for ourselves. Know that joy is your birthright and that you are absolutely deserving of it.

How might you find joy in even small ways today?

Believe in your inherent worthiness.

Your worth isn't something you have to earn; it's there simply because you exist. No matter what you may have believed about this in the past, starting today, you can begin to believe in your immense value, worth and preciousness.

How might you remind yourself of this today?

You are **not** a burden.

You can challenge that voice in your mind that tells you otherwise and keeps you from asking for help, time, or energy from someone else. Your loved ones are happy to be there for you.

How might you allow yourself to ask for what you need today, or enjoy the things that others can do for you?

I believe in you.

I really do. I know this is hard, and I understand. I believe you can get through each day, one at a time, and I believe you can create a beautiful, meaningful life for yourself, whether the pain is part of that or not.

Now, say this to yourself: "I believe in you."

Say it often.

I'm so proud of you.

I really mean that. I know how hard you're trying, and you're doing amazingly well. You've been through things others can't possibly comprehend, and your resilience is so inspiring.

Now, say this to yourself: "I'm so proud of you."

Say it often.

Section 3

Pain & Identity

The pain is real. But so is my resilience, my creativity, my humor, my voice. I am not the pain—I am the person still here beneath it.

You are not the pain, and
the pain is not YOU.

*It can be easy to fall into the trap
of identifying with the pain, but
we can challenge that with this
reminder:*

*Despite how things can feel and
appear, the pain is not who we are,
and it doesn't define us or our
lives. The pain can't touch who we
truly are.*

Living alongside the pain is not the same as giving up or giving in.

Living "alongside" the pain means that you have true agency in your life, and the pain walks alongside you without directing your path.

It means that despite its presence, your life is moving forward. It's a negotiation, not a capitulation.

See the pain as a character in your story. It's not the book.

There is so much more to the story of your life than just the pain.

How might you imagine the pain as a character in your life? What would it look like? See it as one of a cast of many characters that make up the book of you.

Your You-ness is not dimmed by physical limitations.

Your sense of humor, your creativity, your passion, all your skills, talents, and interests. The things you believe in, strive for, and yearn for. Your individuality and your essence.

How might you remind yourself today of the many things that make you who you are?

The pain is not your fault.

Many of us tend to think of the pain as something we did, or something we deserved.

It's not.

How can you release the sense of responsibility for the pain today? How might you let go of self-blame and find compassion instead?

Reclaim your truth. (*Your truth.*)

Many of us have had our experiences invalidated and diminished, impacting our view of ourselves. But here's the thing:

No one knows your truth better than you. Your truth matters. It's real and perfectly valid.

How might you reclaim what's true for you today?

Section 4

Empowerment &
Boundaries

There is strength in setting boundaries. There is power in saying, 'This is what I need.' There is healing in hearing myself say it out loud.

Intentionally protect your peace.

Maybe it's avoiding loud people and places, gossip, or upsetting media. Safeguarding our peace is essential for our nervous system and our ability to self-regulate.

In what ways will you protect your peace today? How might this become an ongoing practice for you?

Intentionally protect your sleep.

Restorative sleep can be a challenge for people living with pain, but it's vital for regenerating in many ways. Perhaps you might avoid commitments late in the day or settle in early with a calming ritual or routine.

How will you protect your precious sleep tonight?

Forgive others for not giving in ways they're not able.

We can offer forgiveness to those who might disappoint us, knowing they truly do care. We might extend a request elsewhere instead and still treasure what those people can freely offer us.

Is there someone you need to forgive? How can you extend compassion and gratitude to them for what they bring to your life?

You can be in charge of
your own story.

*You absolutely do have the power
to redefine your past, present and
future experiences.*

*How might you shape, or reshape,
your story in ways that are more
empowered?*

*Is there a more compassionate way
to reframe your life's story moving
forward?*

Say no when you need to,
without shame, and
without guilt.

*It's not only okay to say no when
you need to; it's an important act
of self-love and self-honoring.*

*How can you cultivate comfort in
saying no, knowing the only
person you're truly obligated to is
yourself?*

Advocate for yourself (and others).

Using our voice, sharing our stories, and asserting ourselves is a valuable and empowering experience. How might you use your voice to assert yourself, and support empowerment for others living with pain? How might this be useful in conversations with providers or others?

Speak your needs to others, knowing you deserve to be heard.

How might you find more confidence speaking to family and friends about your needs?

Is it a boundary? More flexibility when making plans? More help with tasks, errands, transportation or other assistance?

Tell your truth.

*Your truth deserves to be spoken
aloud when needed.*

*Is there something that needs to be
expressed? Is there a conversation
that needs to happen with someone
that will bring resolution or
greater understanding?*

You get to decide how to tell your story.

It's your story, and you are its creator. You can decide to share it from the voice of one who has overcome much and grown wiser, or perhaps one who has found a deeper relationship with yourself through this experience.

From which voice will you tell your story?

Reassess your expectations
of others.

*Discernment is a big part of this
journey, and that includes getting
clearer on what's reasonable to
expect from others, and what's
not. This can help us avoid
disappointment or hidden
resentments.*

*How might you explore
reassessing your expectations of
others today?*

Reassess and redefine your expectations of yourself.

This is an especially important one for those of us who are used to a previous way of going about our days.

How might you soften your expectations for yourself today? How can you offer yourself more flexibility, grace and compassion?

Release any sense of shame or stigma.

Many of us living with chronic pain unconsciously carry some internalized shame and stigma that make us feel "less than."

How might you explore whether that is happening within you? How might you redefine yourself and release shame and stigma?

Section 5

*Adaptability &
Mindset*

*When I can't control the
pain, I shift my attention
to what I **can** control: my
breath, my tone, my
thoughts, my pace.*

Ask yourself: What *is* within my control?

We can easily get stuck in feeling that things are happening "to" us, but we can challenge that by refocusing our energy on what we do have influence over in our lives at this time.

How will you incorporate this question into your day today? How can you ask this of yourself every day?

Pause and observe, rather than reacting.

If we can teach ourselves to pause and observe our internal response to words or events, rather than simply reacting, we give our nervous system time to remain calm.

How might you incorporate this into your day?

Be okay with not knowing.

Uncertainty can feel very uncomfortable for many of us, and that can increase our stress and anxiety. Learning to stay present, and knowing that we simply can't anticipate everything, can help us stay more centered.

How might you sit more comfortably in the space of not knowing?

Ask yourself: What's possible TODAY?

Each new day is a fresh start, and we can assess how we're feeling that day, how our bodies want us to move, and what feels reasonable to undertake. This question helps stem fears of past obstacles that might hinder us from trying something new or trying something again.

What's possible for you today?

Tell yourself: "Well done!" throughout the day.

Maybe a shower is all that happens some days, or making breakfast and washing dishes is the extent of your energy. That's okay. We can still give ourselves credit and praise for doing even one thing from start to finish.

By the way, well done!

Challenge your assumptions.

Assumptions can arise without our awareness, and they can trick us into believing something about ourselves or others.

Is there something you're assuming about yourself or someone else that you could view differently today?

Allow others to help.

Asking for help can be hard enough, but allowing others to help can be equally challenging. It's really okay to let others show their love, and to let them feel needed and appreciated.

How will you grow more comfortable with allowing others to offer and give help?

You *can* choose not to believe your thoughts.

Our minds can convince us of almost anything, but we can choose to ask questions instead and see where there's room for curiosity and inquiry. There may be a new way of seeing things.

How might you observe or reframe your thoughts today?

Ask yourself: What if this were happening *for* you?

It can be natural to see chronic pain as something happening "to" us. But what if it's getting your attention for a reason that's meant to benefit you?

What possibilities might arise from this experience that you hadn't considered before?

Language matters. Use it wisely.

Words have incredible power.

How might you be more intentional with language in shaping your perceptions of yourself, your life, your future, and your world?

Put future goals into present-tense language.

You are entitled to pursue goals and dreams. You can begin manifesting them today by speaking of them in the present tense.

Try saying, "I'm becoming (or doing or learning…)"

What goals can you set into motion today through your words?

Your words really do shape your experiences.

Do you "suffer from" chronic pain, or do you "live with/alongside" it?

How might you redefine your experience of pain, of life, of yourself, with words that embody vitality and empowerment?

Section 6

Daily Living & Gentle Action

Some days I move slowly. Some days I hardly move at all. But even rest can be a sacred act of self-respect.

Ask yourself: What *can* I
do?

*We can easily get caught up in
what we can't do as easily as
before. We can shift that thinking
by asking ourselves a new
question instead and transform
frustration into feelings of success
and accomplishment.*

*What will asking this new
question offer you today?*

One step at a time is
enough.

*Progress can be measured in
increments, and we can feel
satisfaction in achieving any
movement in the right direction.
Allow yourself to find equal
contentment in single steps
forward as you do with many.*

*How might you pace yourself and
your goals with more patience and
love?*

Be intentional about where you direct your energy and focus.

We only have so much energy at a time, and we want to choose wisely what we do with it. Our primary obligation is to ourselves and our well-being, and beyond that, we can direct our energy where it's most constructive and beneficial.

What will this mean for you today?

It's okay to just BE.

We can devote time to ourselves in a state of mindful awareness, just noticing our breath, the room we're in, the sounds we hear, and the sunshine or sound of rain. We can spend more time in this space of "not-doing," knowing it's time well spent.

What will this look like for you today?

Allow yourself to slow down *even more.*

We sometimes feel we need to accomplish as much as we can while we have energy and stamina. But if we slow down, we can complete our tasks with more presence and awareness and go about our day with a sense of gentleness.

How will you let yourself slow down more today?

Allow for breaks and time for rest.

This is such an important part of getting in touch with our needs and listening to our bodies' wisdom. We might have "powered through" in the past, but that mindset doesn't serve us any longer.

How can you listen to your body today and allow for rest when you need it?

Let a friend tell you about their day.

This can be a lovely way to connect with someone, and it can serve as a welcome distraction from our cares, thoughts, and pain.

Whom might you like to check in with today so you can hear about their day?

Discover healthy and calming distractions.

Perhaps it's knitting or reading a book with a nice cup of tea. A new sketchbook, a journal, some watercolor paints…something to spark your creative flow…

What kind of healthy, calming distraction feels appealing to you today?

Wear clothing that feels comfortable on your body. Think easy, soft, loose.

Tight, constricting clothing is not a friend to chronic pain, and besides, this is our new era of softening and easing in many ways. You can still have personal style and flair while honoring your comfort. What will that look like today?

Nourish your body with beautiful, healing food.

Part of honoring ourselves is knowing that our bodies need and deserve food that nourishes and heals. Make your meals beautiful, even the simpler ones. It can be a sacred act of reverence and joy.

How will you make your meals beautiful today?

Listen to music that
soothes and inspires you.

*Music can lift us up, soothe our
soul, and inspire us to carry on
and thrive. It can take us out of
the busy space in our minds and
transport us to other realms.*

*What music is calling to you
today?*

Try at least one new thing today.

There is so much in life that we can tap into, and trying something new keeps us vibrant and growing.

A new language, a new form of safe movement, a new musical instrument, a new recipe...

What new thing sounds fun and engaging for you today?

Simplify. Delegate.

It can be easy to feel overwhelmed when living with chronic pain. Finding ways to simplify our surroundings and our routines can help, and delegating some tasks to others can relieve some of the burdens of everyday life.

What are some ways you can begin to simplify and delegate today?

Approach the day with curiosity.

Each new day is a new opportunity, filled with new possibilities. All we need to do is be present and open to them.

What might you do, try, reclaim, or redefine today? What surprises may be in store?

Create a space that nourishes and sustains you.

Your space is your sanctuary. An environment that calms and supports you and reflects beauty and peace can be so soothing and uplifting. Even a small tabletop is a good start.

How might you create a space of solace for yourself today?

Every baby step is a milestone.

We can choose to reshape our definition of "progress" to include celebrating the small wins alongside the big ones. We can enjoy that sense of pride and accomplishment that makes us feel more self-sufficient.

How might you celebrate the small wins today?

Melt into it. Lean in.

Rather than resisting what you feel, try melting into it more deeply. We can learn from our discomfort if we approach it as an opportunity to learn something about ourselves.

Can you befriend uncomfortable feelings today? What are they wanting you to know?

Engage and activate your senses.

Deep observation can bring us into the present moment and distract us from the pain. Sights and sounds, holding a polished stone or stroking a pet's soft fur, lighting a scented candle, sipping mint tea…these can activate a calming effect on our nervous system.

What can you perceive now?

Nourish your mind, spirit, and soul.

We are deeply complex and multifaceted beings, and sometimes pain can make us focus on our physical aspect at the expense of our mental and spiritual sides.

What is your spirit craving today? How can you fuel your inquisitive mind? What does your soul need to feel grounded today?

Section 7

*Purpose, Growth, &
Forward Motion*

*I used to think healing
meant going back to who I
was. Now I know it means
becoming someone new—
someone softer, deeper,
and still whole.*

Imagine this experience as an opportunity for growth.

What if this experience were a means to evolve and grow into who we're meant to become now? What if this weren't just a collapse of what we knew before, but an opportunity to reclaim our lives in ways we never would have otherwise?

Trust the process. (And it *is* a process.)

We don't have to have all the answers right now. This is a process, and growth takes time and patience. Each day, whether you can see it or not, you are becoming more deeply acquainted with yourself and your higher purpose.

How can you allow for trust in this process today?

Ask yourself: What might your new purpose be?

Allow yourself to envision the new purpose that this experience is guiding you toward. Chances are, you already have an inkling. Chronic pain, and all that comes with it, can be our teacher if we let it.

What has this experience taught you so far? Where might it lead you?

Be willing to turn your gaze *forward*.

Rather than focusing on what our lives looked like before chronic pain, allow yourself to believe that you have more unwritten chapters in your story, whether you can see the pages yet or not.

What might be waiting for you in your next chapter?

Release clinging to what
was.

*Change is the one constant in life,
and we can choose to embrace it
rather than resist it. Letting go of
past versions of ourselves allows
space for who we're meant to
become next, and there might just
be beautiful surprises there.*

*What does releasing the past look
like for you today?*

Let grief arise when it needs to.

Sitting with our grief for what was and what we expected life to bring us is an important step in moving forward. Allow the grief to arise, sit with it in compassion, and let it move through you with love. Grief is a natural part of this process, and it's okay to feel it.

Feel *all* the things.

The impact of chronic pain can bring many emotions to the surface. Each one deserves our attention and our love, and each has something to teach us. It's okay to feel sad, angry, frustrated, happy, curious and bored.

What if there were no "bad" feelings?

Surrender is allowing for what *is*.

It's about allowing. Allowing for what you feel, allowing what life is bringing to you right now, allowing for things to be exactly as they are. It's the absence of resistance.

How can you soften into peace and surrender today?

Believe that there is a higher purpose involved.

Life holds so much mystery, and there are forces beyond our comprehension and understanding.

What if we hand over control to that higher purpose and let it guide us forward?

What might that look like for you today?

Resilience grows by the day. (And sometimes by the hour, and sometimes by the minute.)

What if we believed that our resilience is growing with every breath we take? Even on the hardest days, we are persevering, and that is pure resilience.

Believe.

Embody goodwill toward yourself (and others).

When we come from a place of peace, we can see the best in ourselves and in others. We can choose to let go of harboring criticism, resentment and doubt in the pursuit of a peaceful spirit.

How might you choose kindness today?

Nourish your sense of curiosity about the world.

There is so much out there in the world to learn about. Even if we find ourselves at home most of the time, we can remember the world is still ours to discover.

Cultures, traditions, wildlife, science, the stars and planets...what's piquing your interest today?

Replenish your soul with things that uplift and inspire you.

Spending time in nature, seeing a ballet, watching the sun rise…

These can bring us a sense of awe and wonder that nourishes us on such a deep level.

How can you replenish your soul today?

Be open to what life is calling you to now.

Maybe it's a new event awaiting you at the library, or a book club that you can easily access. Life is calling you to new things, new people, and a new purpose. It's not over yet....

Keep an ear to the wind...listen for the things calling to you now. Are you listening?

Additional Resources

The WordWise Project
thewordwiseproject.com

U.S. Pain Foundation
usspainfoundation.org

American Chronic Pain Association
acpanow.org

International Association for the
Study of Pain (IASP)
iasp-pain.org

Acknowledgements

To my beloved family and treasured friends who stood by me and lifted me up during the most difficult time in my life, and ever since…

To my precious daughter, whose love and incredible support have meant everything…

To the beautiful, amazing, newer people in my life who came along as I listened to what life was calling me to next…

To the best little library I know, which has been the epicenter of so much new possibility and purpose for me…

To my incredible and supportive providers, without whom I couldn't have gotten where I am now, in so many ways…

To my precious, sweet kitties, who give me so much joy and love…

…I offer a deep bow of gratitude and my eternal thanks and love.

About the Author

Julie Gruber is a former educator, coach, writer, artist, and mom. In 2016, she developed a chronic pain condition that changed her life in ways she couldn't have foreseen. Since then, she has transformed this experience into a new way of living and being.

In 2025, she started The WordWise Project, which aims to help others living alongside chronic pain reclaim their lives and redefine their experience through empowerment, resilience, and creative inspiration.

She lives in Michigan with her three cats, numerous books, sketchpads, and her stash of homemade chocolate.

To read more of Julie's work and get updates on her upcoming books and other projects, you can find her on Substack.